THE TIMEWARP TRIALS

BOUDICCA
GUILTY OR INNOCENT?

Stewart Ross

illustrated by Élisabeth Eudes-Pascal

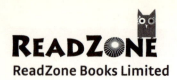

ReadZone Books Limited

First published in this edition 2017

© copyright in the text Stewart Ross 2011
© copyright in this edition ReadZone Books 2017

First published 2011 by Evans Brothers Ltd

The right of the Author to be identified as the Author of this work
has been asserted by the Author in accordance with the Copyright,
Designs and Patents Act 1988.

Printed in Malta by Melita Press

British Library Cataloguing in Publication Data (CIP) is available
for this title.

ISBN 978-1-78322-634-4

Visit our website: www.readzonebooks.com

THE TIMEWARP TRIALS

BOUDICCA
GUILTY OR INNOCENT?

Stewart Ross

illustrated by Élisabeth Eudes-Pascal

The High Court of History

Witness

WITNESS BOX

Defence lawyer,
Mr Leroy Williams

JURY

In the beginning…

DOCTOR DAVID GIBBON WAS WORRIED. 'It's Horatio,' he explained to his wife Emelda. 'Now that his High Court of History has been so successful, I'm afraid he'll go and do something daft.'

'Daft?'

'Well, you know, put someone on trial without asking me first. Someone entirely unsuitable. He almost did it last time. You know he wanted to put George Washington in the dock?'

'Good heavens!' exclaimed Mrs Gibbon. Being a sensible, no-nonsense sort of woman, she suggested that her husband act immediately. 'Go round to Horatio's place at once, David, and talk to him face to face. I know he'll listen to you.'

'We hope,' muttered David, going to get his car keys.

Three hours later, Doc Gibbon, the leading historian of his time, was sitting in the vast kitchen of Newton Hall nursing a mug of steaming tea. Seated at the opposite side of the table, Professor Horatio Geekmeister leaned forward eagerly.

'I'm so glad you've come, David,' he was saying. 'I've started making preparations for the next trial in the High Court of History – but I'm having a few problems and I need your help.'

'Very kind of you, Horatio. I'll do what I can,' Doc David said. 'And, er, who are you thinking of bringing back from a scrap of DNA this time?'

Professor Geekmeister gave one of his odd little smiles. 'I think it's time we had a woman, don't you?'

'An excellent idea. But who?'

'I'd like to see if my technique works on DNA over a thousand years old, so I've chosen Boudicca.'

'Boudicca the Celtic queen?' exclaimed David. 'Impossible!'

'Why? A great subject: was the Queen of the Iceni tribe a cold-blooded mass murderer or a heroic freedom fighter?'

Doc David took a deep breath. 'Great idea, Horatio, but it just won't work.'

'Explain yourself. You just want to spoil my fun, don't you?'

'No, Horatio. The problem is getting the DNA. There's nothing left of Queen Boudicca except the name, and there's even disagreement about that. Some people still think she's not Boudicca at all, but Boadicea.'

Professor Geekmeister leapt to his feet. 'That's where you're wrong, my dear David. Not about the name but about the DNA. A grave has been found, a mysterious grave!'

'Under platform nine at King's Cross Station, as the rumour says?'

'Of course not! It's in a field near Leicester. Come on, I'll take you there right now!

Dr David Gibbon stared down into the wide pit that Geekmeister's archaeologists had dug. The skeleton, excellently preserved in the muddy clay, was certainly that of a woman. A tall one, too, fitting the description of Boudicca by the Roman historian Dio. The precious ornaments buried with her, including a huge gold necklace, suggested a person of great importance.

Most convincing, however, were the two smaller skeletons lying beside the larger one.

'Well?' enquired Professor Geekmeister, almost falling into the pit in his excitement. 'It has to be her, doesn't it?'

Being a professional historian, Doc David was more cautious. 'It might be the rebel queen and the two daughters who died with her. The design of the necklace seems about right, and the way it's decorated, too. Yes, it may actually be Boudicca. But there's no way of telling.'

'Oh yes there is,' cackled Geekmeister. 'Look at all those lovely bones! Enough DNA to make an army. I shall bring her back from the dead! I shall recreate Queen Boudicca!'

The Accused

TO THE ASTONISHMENT of the entire world, Professor Geekmeister was right. He really had found Boudicca's grave. Using his secret process, he brought her and two others from that time back to life. When all was ready, he summoned the High Court of History to meet for a third time.

The four children on the jury were delighted, especially Jasmine and Tom. The last trials – of Henry VIII and Guy Fawkes – had been international TV successes, making the school children minor celebrities. The judge, The Honourable Ms Winifred Wigmore, had become famous, too. The lawyers for the prosecution and defence, Miss Tankia Bessant and Mr Leroy Williams, had been invited to take part in a televised dance competition. Even the court clerk, Mr George S. Cribble, had been asked for his autograph when he was out shopping in Sainsbury's.

Because the court was now so well known, Professor Geekmeister gave all who sat in it a long lecture about their responsibilities. They must ignore the cameras, never show off and, above all, they must be one hundred per cent honest and fair. The life – or rather the second life – of the accused person depended on it.

Not that Boudicca made things easy for herself. On the way into the courtroom she screamed at the press and TV crews, kicked and bit the security men, and used her waist-long red hair as a rope to try to strangle a cleaning lady. Still struggling, she was hauled into the chamber and into the dock. Even then another half hour passed before she had calmed down enough for Judge Wigmore to begin addressing her.

'Would you kindly tell the court your name, madam?' she began.

Boudicca glared at her in silence.

'Your name, please!'

Again Boudicca said nothing.

'Listen,' the judge said in a tone she might normally have used with a five-year-old, 'what I have to say is very important. Professor Geekmeister has kindly brought you back from the dead–'

At this point she was interrupted by a howl that might have come from a thousand starving wolves. 'Owwww!' wailed Boudicca, on and on. 'I would rather still be dead than be a Roman!'

A light seemed to spring on behind Judge Wigmore's eyes. 'Roman?' she enquired. 'You are not Roman. I am not Roman. And this is not Rome.'

It took about thirty seconds for the words to sink in. When they did, Boudicca swished back the waterfall of her hair and asked in a much quieter voice, 'Did you say this was not Rome – sir?'

Professor Geekmeister was following events on TV back in Newton Hall. Boudicca's ignorance alarmed him. He had programmed her

in the same way as Henry VIII and Guy Fawkes, and they had turned out alright. What had gone wrong? Maybe the warrior queen was simply not very bright? The professor twisted his fingers anxiously. Oh dear, he thought, I hope she doesn't spoil it all by flying off the handle again!

Meanwhile, Ms Wigmore explained that she was in fact not a man but a woman wearing unusual headgear. She then told Boudicca that there had been a serious misunderstanding about Rome. They were now in the 21st century and

the Roman Empire had collapsed over 1,400 years before. Boudicca let out a whoop of joy.

After explaining the purpose of the High Court of History and how it worked, the judge went back to the beginning and asked the accused to state her name. Boudicca. Good. The judge then said she was there because as Queen of the Iceni she had been responsible for mass murder and other cruelties, and she now stood accused of those crimes.

'What is the cowardly charge – My Lady?' interrupted Boudicca, remembering just in time to use the correct language of the court.

'You are accused of being a butcher,' replied Ms Wigmore bluntly.

'A stall keeper? A mere meat chopper?' spat Boudicca, as if she was about to explode again.

'No. Not a cutter of animal meat. You are accused of the cold-blooded mass murder of innocent men, women and children. How do you plead?'

Boudicca laughed. It was a harsh, rasping noise; truly a sound from another age. 'I plead not guilty!' she boomed. 'I was a freedom fighter, never a butcher!'

Through all this, Tom, the schoolboy jury-member with black-framed glasses, had been just a little bit frightened. Henry VIII had been full of bluster and Guy Fawkes had been a bit sinister, but neither of them had been anything like this. She was incredible, this Boudicca woman. Such fiery energy! Such passion and power! Tom nudged Jasmine, who was sitting beside him. 'Scary, eh?' he muttered.

His friend didn't move. Without taking her eyes off Boudicca for a split second, she simply mouthed, 'Terrifying! Really, really terrifying!'

The Prosecution

THE RAVEN-HAIRED, hook-nosed Tankia Bessant was a no-nonsense sort of person. With her, what you saw was what you got – and she wished everyone else was like that, too. When prosecuting in court she did not care one jot who the accused was – king, queen, bishop, soldier, street sweeper – she treated them all exactly the same. And that is why Professor Geekmeister had chosen her to be the chief prosecuting lawyer in the High Court of History.

Like all good lawyers, Miss Bessant did her homework extremely thoroughly. She read all she could about the Boudicca case, which was not very much, and also spoke to several experts. So now, as she stood up and walked towards the jury in her clicking, hard-heeled shoes, she knew exactly what she was about.

Watching the lawyer coming towards her with precise, determined steps, almost like a machine, Jasmine felt comfortable again. When someone as powerful as Miss Tankia Bessant was around, everyone was safe – apart from those who were guilty.

'Respected citizens of the jury,' began the lawyer, 'for many, many years the accused,

who stands before you in the dock, has been
something of a hero. Indeed, if you travel to
the great city of London you will find there a
magnificent statue of her. It stands beside the
River Thames, next to the Houses of Parliament,
and shows the accused in a war chariot with her
two daughters.

'The Celtic name "Boudicca" means
"Victory", so the modern version of her name
is "Victoria". That's why the Victorians admired
her quite so much. To them she represented
battling Britain.'

Miss Bessant turned to face the judge. 'Yet I find it strange, My Lady, to find her statue in London. Very strange indeed.'

She turned back towards the jury. 'Do you know what the accused did to London? She ravaged it. She smashed and burned it. She and her barbaric army slaughtered every citizen they could get their hands on. They hacked them and hanged them, spiked them, set fire to them and crucified them. Thousands they killed, thousands upon thousands.

'Was this the work of a hero? Do we admire people who behave like that, people who today would be found guilty of war crimes? No, good citizens of the jury, we do not. There is only one word for those who carry out such vile and unnecessary acts, and that word is "butcher"!

'Ladies, gentlemen and children of the jury, as I will show you, Queen Boudicca of the Iceni is guilty. One hundred per cent guilty of butchery.'

Tom and Jasmine looked at each other open-mouthed. They had never heard Miss Bessant like this before, so fired up, so passionate. What she said about Boudicca was a bit of a shock, too. Jasmine's teacher had said she really admired the ancient queen because she had showed that there was nothing women could not do. She even got the whole class making Celtic chariots out of wire, matchboxes and papier maché.

Now, after Miss Bessant's speech, Jasmine found herself having second thoughts.

'You heard what I said to the jury, Boudicca?' the prosecutor asked as she walked slowly over to the dock.

Tall and upright, the Queen of the Iceni looked scornfully down on her questioner.

'My hearing is that of a warrior,' she replied. 'As keen as any doe's.'

'And you understood my words?'

'My mind is that of a warrior, sharp and quick like an arrow. You told those common people over there – your jury – of the mighty blows I struck for freedom. But you told them lies, too.'

Miss Bessant raised a single neat eyebrow. 'Lies, eh? How does killing thousands of people strike a blow for freedom?'

Boudicca looked confused. 'How? How? What do you mean?'

'During your revolt, you and your army slew most of the population of London, as well as of Camulodunum, which we call Colchester, and of Verulamium, known to us as St Albans. What does all that blood have to do with freedom?'

Boudicca drew herself up so she looked even taller than before and stretched out her bare arms before her.

'What I did was no butchery!' she exclaimed. The power of her voice made the TV pictures of the trial go wobbly all around the world.

'I did not kill to protect the honour of my noble family, nor to get my stolen lands back, nor to recover my wealth. I struck a blow for liberty! And for revenge! Revenge against those who had flogged me and against those who had mistreated my daughters so horribly! I killed, yes I killed. But I killed the invader, the unwanted, cruel stranger! I killed to set my people free!'

The jury felt battered, as if they had been standing on the sea front during a storm. So much emotion, so much power – it was all utterly exhausting. Judge Wigmore felt in need of a rest, too, and ordered the court to break for lunch.

When the trial resumed, Miss Bessant went on the counter-attack. She agreed that the queen and her family had been badly treated, but that was no reason for wholesale slaughter. And what was this "freedom" she spoke of? Freedom to live outside Roman civilization, with its law and order and prosperity – was that freedom? Freedom to return to the old Celtic ways, the cruel ceremonies, the endless fighting and the barbaric poverty – is that what she wanted for her people?

At first Boudicca did not reply. When she did, she simply said, 'You do not, cannot understand. It was a matter of the heart.'

'Crucifying people was a matter of the heart, was it?' Miss Bessant retorted. 'Let's hear someone else's views about that. Mr Cribble, call Terran the Trader please.'

Terran the
Trader

'WHO?' JASMINE WHISPERED to Tom
as soon as the name of the prosecution witness
was called.

Tom shrugged. 'No idea. Never heard of him.
Or her.'

Nor had anyone else before Professor
Geekmeister had brought him back to life.
The brilliant scientist managed it by using a
piece of thigh bone found deep in the ground
near Tower Hill Underground Station, London.
Having resurrected the man's body, he used
another of his special processes to programme
the witness's speech into more-or-less-modern
English. That done, the professor questioned his
creation and learned that he was Terran
the Trader, a London merchant from the
first century AD.

A small man wearing a spotless white toga,
Terran walked into the court with quick, neat
steps. Once he had taken his position in the
witness box, Miss Bessant got him to explain
his background. He had lived in Londinium –
London – with his wife and family at the time
of the emperor Nero. Although Britain had
only recently come under Roman rule, London

was rapidly growing into a large and prosperous town. Terran made good money importing stone jars of wine from the south. He had become friends with some of the city's Roman administrators and had hopes of becoming a Roman citizen himself one day.

But it was not to be.

'And would you be so good as to explain to the court why you never became a Roman citizen, Mr Terran?' asked Tankia Bessant.

The trader looked across at Boudicca. 'Because of that woman over there!' he replied in a high, shrill voice. 'She and her fellow barbarians ruined everything!'

'Traitor!' hissed Boudicca, raising her arm and throwing an imaginary spear at him across the court. 'Rome-lover! Turncoat!'

'Hideous barbarian!' shouted Terran back at her, shaking his fist.

Judge Wigmore's voice rose above the din. 'Boudicca! Terran! Be quiet both of you! You will respect this court, understand?'

Terran nodded, but Boudicca simply shrugged and stood staring proudly before her. The judge sighed. 'If you want the court – indeed, the whole world – to hear your side of the story, Boudicca, then I advise you to play by our rules.'

When still the haughty queen did not move, Ms Wigmore turned to the court sergeant. 'Sergeant Vanwall, kindly get your men to release the accused from the dock and take her down to the cells for a few days.'

Ms Wigmore turned to the jury. 'If at the end of that time, members of the jury, the accused will still not cooperate, then I shall have no choice but to hand her back to Professor Geekmeister. I apologise for wasting your time.'

As the judge was speaking, Boudicca had turned very slowly to look at the jury. Her fierce blue-green eyes, the colour and shape of a cat's, met those of Jasmine and for a few seconds she and the schoolgirl stared at each other. What Jasmine did next, she was never able to explain. It just happened. Gazing into Boudicca's eyes, held there as if by a magic spell, she opened her lips and mouthed silently, 'Please stay!'

Boudicca breathed deeply though her nose and looked away. Then, as Sergeant Vanwall and his security men advanced towards her, she raised her hand like a traffic policeman.

'Stop!' she commanded. 'I will do what the court wishes. For the sake of my daughters.'

'Your daughters?' enquired Judge Wigmore.

'That child over there – the girl in the jury – she reminds me of my own children. So, as she wishes, I stay here. I will cooperate.'

'Thank you,' said the judge. 'You may continue your questions, Miss Bessant.'

Jasmine hardly heard what was said over the next few hours. Why had she done that? she kept asking herself. What was it about that strange fiery woman from another time, another world even, that had so fascinated her?

'Still find her scary?' Tom asked during the tea break.

'Scary? Yes, scary and, well, sort of weird,' Jasmine replied. 'Did you see what happened?'

'You mean you asking her to stay?'

Jasmine nodded.

'Sure, I saw,' said Tom. 'Thought you were just trying to help the judge.'

'Maybe I was, but she's still weird.'

Tom shrugged. 'I know. That's what makes it so fantastic. Gonna be really difficult when it comes to the decision time, guilty or not guilty.'

Jasmine nodded. 'Yes, really, really difficult.'

By the time Miss Bessant had finished questioning Terran the Trader, however, it all seemed a lot less difficult. The merchant and his family had been in London when the city was sacked by Boudicca and her horde. He had

wanted to leave with the army of Governor Suetonius but his wife had been too ill to travel and his children refused to go without her.

When Boudicca's Iceni and Trinovantes tribesmen poured into the city, Terran had barricaded his house to keep them out. It was a useless move.

For two days bands of drunken warriors wandered the streets. Deaf to pleas for mercy, they murdered in the most vile ways anyone they found, Briton or Roman. No prisoners were taken. On the second evening, Terran had crept out in disguise to look for food and water. Sneaking past the main square, the forum, he had seen Boudicca with his own eyes.

'Yes,' he explained, 'I was an eyewitness. She had been watching a group of London women being killed by torture. At no time had she objected. Actually, she seemed to enjoy it and even joined in herself every now and again.'

'And after that?' asked Miss Bessant, her face long and serious.

'After that she stood on a ruined pillar and screamed at the crowd milling around her. "Fire!" she yelled. "Burn down this foreign town!

Every house, every temple, everything must be reduced to ashes! Burn! Burn! Burn!" She grabbed a brand from the fire and rushed towards the house nearest to her. Others followed her example. Before long the whole of London was a roaring inferno.'

Terran explained how he had tried to return to his house but had been beaten back by the flames. Taking refuge in a cellar, he had died when the building above him collapsed.

Tankia Bessant waited for Terran's story to sink in before saying, 'But Boudicca and her army would accuse you of siding with the enemy, Terran. The Romans were the conquerors and you and all the other people of London had joined with them. They would say that you deserved your fate for being a traitor. Were you?'

The question made Terran almost jump with anger. 'I sided with civilization,' he squawked. 'I sided with Rome against barbarity, against the sort of things Boudicca did. Sure, the Romans were cruel compared with you people today but at least they had proper laws and courts and schools and books and roads and coins and culture… Don't you see, they were the future.

That woman over there in the dock, that wild thing, she was the past.'

'And not a freedom fighter?' asked Miss Bessant, raising an eyebrow.

'Freedom fighter?' cried Terran. 'Freedom fighter? The only freedom she wanted was the freedom to rule her own paltry little kingdom in the way she wanted. Without law. She wanted power for herself, that's all.'

'And to get that she slaughtered all those thousands?'

'Yes. I saw her, don't forget. I saw her by the firelight. I saw the look in her eyes, the look of a mad woman, the evil glare of a butcher!'

Tankia Bessant turned to the jury. 'Ladies, gentlemen and children, you have heard all the evidence you need. Only one verdict is possible: Butcher Boudicca is guilty!'

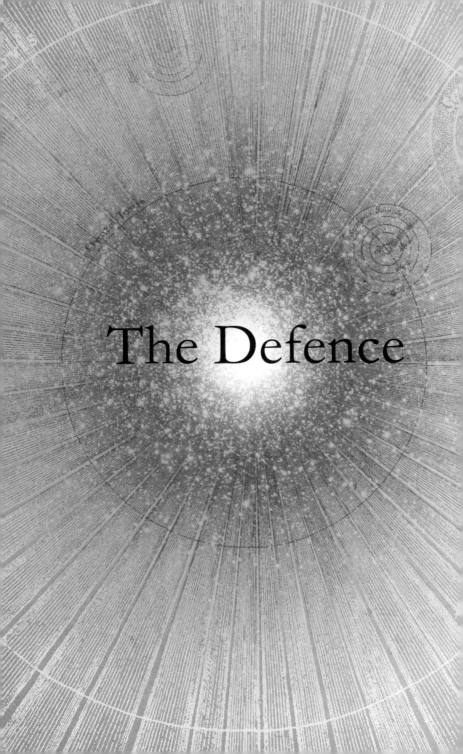

The Defence

'SO WHAT DO YOU THINK old Leroy is going to come up with to prove she's innocent?' Tom asked the other children when they were sitting in the jury lounge during a break.

Everyone looked at Jasmine. 'Come on, Jaz,' said Tom. 'You're the one she likes, her favourite. What's so good about Boudicca?'

Jasmine wrinkled up her face. 'Oh come on, Tom! That's not fair! I just said she was weird, that's all. You know, strange. Different.'

Tom took a swig out of the can he was holding. 'Yes, but they're all like that, aren't they? I mean everyone we've seen from the past is a bit odd. They don't think like us, do they?'

'No, I know that. But Boudicca's really, really peculiar, isn't she?'

'Maybe. But that's because she's from so long ago. We have to try to understand, don't we? Remember what the prof said about being fair.'

'OK, don't go on about it. Perhaps you're right. But she's still like an alien.'

The conversation was cut short by George S. Cribble, the court clerk, who at that moment came into the room and asked them all to return to their places.

Having defended Henry VIII and Guy Fawkes, defence lawyer Leroy Williams was used to tricky cases. He knew exactly how to show that the ancient British queen was not a butcher – someone who killed simply for the sake of killing – but a typical warrior of her time. He also planned to show the jury that she had been forced to fight because of Roman cruelty against her, her family and her people.

'Boudicca, Your Majesty,' he began, 'would you please tell the court why you raised your people in revolt against the Romans?'

The accused woman looked at him in surprise. 'You don't know?'

Mr Williams smiled. 'Yes I know, Your Majesty. But there are some here who do not.'

The frown slipped from the stately queen's face. 'Ah! I led my people, the Iceni, to regain their freedom. When our neighbours, the Trinovantes, heard of our rebellion, they joined us along with others from every corner of our sacred island. We all had one wish, to drive the invader into the sea, to wash ourselves clean in his blood–'

'Yes, yes,' intervened her lawyer hastily. 'We'll come on to the blood later, Your Majesty.

For the moment would you say exactly what turned you against the Romans?'

'When my husband, the noble Prasutagus, was taken by the gods—'

'Taken by the gods?'

'When he died, Mr Williams,' explained Boudicca scornfully. 'When he was taken by the gods he ordered that our kingdom be shared between the emperor of Rome and our two daughters, Arian and Gara.'

'He wanted the Emperor Nero to have part of his kingdom?'

'Yes. We were allies of Rome at that time. Like the foolish child with the adder, we trusted them.'

Boudicca went on to explain how her husband's will had been ignored and the Romans had seized her husband's entire kingdom, carrying off its wealth and taxing its people.

'And you and your daughters,' asked Leroy Williams, 'how were you treated?'

Once again, as if gathering herself for action, the queen drew in a long breath through her nose before speaking. 'What those vile men did to Arian and Gara can never be forgiven or forgotten. Death is the only punishment those monsters deserve.'

With a swift movement the queen cast off her long woollen cloak and let it fall to the floor beside her. 'And me, a queen, a woman of noble blood,' she continued in a voice that became louder and harsher with every syllable, 'this royal lady they dared to whip most cruelly. See!'

As she spoke she lifted her shirt clean over her head. There she stood, bare from the waist up, totally unashamed. The loud gasp of surprise that greeted her behaviour quickly turned to one of dismay. Tom and Jasmine stared in horror. It was not the queen's nakedness that shocked them but the state of her body. Across her white skin, back and front, dozens of broad red scars rose in hideous, scarlet ridges.

Later, when he had got over his surprise, Tom wondered how on earth Professor Geekmeister had managed it. How had he used the DNA from a dead woman to recreate the same person a few months before she died? As with Henry VIII and Guy Fawkes, the professor was able to choose the exact age at which a person would resurrect. Amazing!

Back in court, Boudicca's harsh tones broke the silence. 'That was the gift Rome gave me to mark my husband's death. Scars to go with my tears.'

Judge Wigmore decided to intervene before the fiery queen did anything even more outrageous. 'The court would be grateful if the accused covered herself immediately and offered us no more intimate revelations.'

When the queen was fully dressed again, Leroy Williams resumed the defence. 'Ladies and gentlemen and children of the jury, I apologise for that display, but I am sure you realise why it was necessary.'

Jasmine, Tom and the other two children in the jury nodded as the lawyer walked slowly towards them.

'The accused, a proud queen, had suffered most terribly. Her lands had been seized, her daughters ravaged and herself flogged.

'Before his death, King Prasutagus and Queen Boudicca had worked with the Romans in good faith. Their reward? Treachery and unspeakable cruelty. No, it was not a thirst for blood, simple butchery, that drove the queen to revolt. It was desperation. What else could the proud and noble woman have done? There was no law court to take her case to. Should she have gone on her knees before the conquerors and thanked them for their cruelty? I think not!'

Mr Williams walked back to the judge. 'My Lady, I would now like to call my witness, Governor Gaius Suetonius Paulinus.'

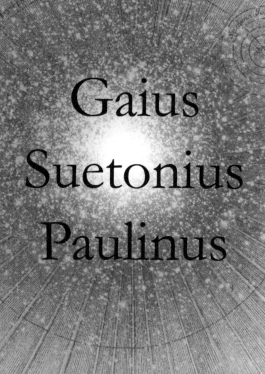

Gaius
Suetonius
Paulinus

WHEN HE WAS EIGHT YEARS OLD,
in Miss Denton's class, Tom had drawn a
picture of a Roman soldier: tall and muscular,
he wore a smart uniform under shiny armour;
his hair was close-cropped, his eyes small, his
mouth just a pencil line. Now, looking at
Gaius Suetonius Paulinus, Tom felt as if he
were looking at his own picture come to life.
The governor was exactly as everyone
imagined a Roman to be: tough, efficient,
hard as the steel of the helmet he carried
under his right arm.

Leroy Williams began by getting Suetonius,
as he was known, to explain to the court who
he was and what his job had been in Britain. His
task was simple, he said. As governor he was
charged with bringing the whole island under
the rule of the emperor. When asked how this
was to be done, his answer was as blunt as it was
shocking: brute force.

'Brute force,' repeated Mr Williams,
pretending to think carefully about the phrase.
'Brute force… mmmm. Did it work, Governor?'

'Never failed. The only thing that those
barbarians understand.'

'Did Boudicca understand it? Your brute force drove the Iceni and their queen to a violent rebellion.'

Without changing his expression, Suetonius replied, 'You mean the trouble we had with that woman over there? That was nothing really. Just gave us an opportunity to tighten our grip and wipe out some of the troublemakers.'

'But it is said that Emperor Nero considered abandoning Britain altogether when he heard of Boudicca's success.'

'I know. He always was a bit feeble, that Nero chap. Always fiddling around, never getting on with things.'

Leroy Williams smiled. 'And you did get on with things?'

'Of course. After I'd smashed the rebel barbarians and killed as many of them as I could– '

'I gather their army was a bit, well, disorganised. Women and children and babies all mixed up with the men.'

Suetonius smiled coldly. 'That's right. Such hard work, slaughtering. Gave you arm ache. Difficult not to slip over, too, with all that blood about the place.'

The lawyer turned to the jury. 'It seems, ladies, gentlemen and children, that the Romans were just as keen on butchery as the Britons. It was a bloodthirsty age, wasn't it?'

He turned back to the witness. 'Governor Suetonius, were you shocked or horrified at what Boudicca's forces had done to the towns they had captured?'

'Shocked? Horrified? Of course not! They were just doing what we did. All's fair in war, you know. No time for sentiment, especially where barbarians are concerned.'

Mr Williams frowned. 'But the rebels crucified innocent people, Governor!'

Suetonius looked surprised. 'Really? Typical barbarians, always copying our ways even when they pretended to hate us! Crucifixion was our method of execution. They picked it up from us.'

'You used it?'

'Hundreds of times, possibly even thousands. After the rebellion I decided to teach the barbarians a lesson they'd never forget. Just in case they ever thought of challenging Rome again.'

'And what did you do?' The lawyer's voice sounded unusually tired.

'Oh, the usual thing. Burned villages, confiscated all the land, killed the inhabitants. It was up to the soldiers themselves how they chose to do it. Some liked to torture and crucify, others just stabbed and chopped. All a matter of taste, really–'

'Enough!' Leroy Williams suddenly cried. 'We have heard enough, Governor Suetonius.

Thank you. I do have just one last question for you, though.'

'Yes?'

'Would you describe your work as "butchery"?'

The witness thought for a moment. 'Mmmm, on reflection I suppose the answer is "yes", if you mean by "butchery" deliberate killing. Yes, I suppose in doing my duty I was a bit of a butcher. The only thing barbarians understand, you know.'

After Gaius Suetonius Paulinus had left the court, Judge Wigmore gave everyone a long break. Sitting in the jury lounge, all Jasmine could say was, 'I'm so glad I was born nowadays and not then.'

Tom nodded. 'Funny, isn't it? At school you learn about the Romans building roads and bridges and all that sort of thing, but never about their vicious side.'

'Yeah, true. Not that Boudicca was any better, was she?'

'Hardly.'

Leroy Williams finished his case for the defence by explaining that in a violent age

Boudicca had simply behaved as others did. In trying to set her people free, she had given the Romans a taste of their own medicine. She was, he concluded, not a butcher but a tough fighter for freedom. A hero, really.

'So, members of the jury, the verdict is clear. I am sure that you will conclude that Boudicca, a great British hero, is not guilty.'

He makes it sound so easy! thought Tom, gazing over to where Boudicca stood, still and solemn as a statue, on the other side of the court. What an unusual woman she was! Guilty or not, she was certainly impressive.

'Right,' said Judge Wigmore after Leroy Williams had sat down, 'ladies, gentlemen and children of the jury, it is now over to you. You have heard the evidence presented by Miss Bessant and Mr Williams, and you must retire to reach a verdict. I can give you no advice other than to take your time, consider carefully and be prepared to change your mind.

'Finally, remember that if you find Boudicca guilty, she will spend the rest of her second life behind bars. If, on the other hand, you find her not guilty, she will be free – although at first she may find the ways of the 21st century a bit difficult to grasp.

'I now ask you to retire from the court and begin your deliberations.'

Dear Reader,

YOU are a member of the jury!

You were one of the two children sitting behind Jasmine and Tom.

If you go to my website **www.stewartross.com**, you can get in touch and tell me your decision: Boudicca, guilty or not guilty of being a cold-blooded mass murderer – a butcher?

I will write back and let you know how others have voted. And when we have enough votes, I'll put a page on my website announcing the verdict: Boudicca, guilty or innocent?

I do hope you enjoyed the book. If you did, you might like the others in the Timewarp Trials series.

Best wishes

Boudicca's revolt

55 BC	Julius Caesar's first visit to Britain.
43 AD	Emperor Claudius launches a full-scale Roman invasion of Britain.
58	Gaius Suetonius Paulinus appointed governor of Britain.
60	Death of King Prasutagus of the Iceni tribe.
c. 61	Revolt of Boudicca, Queen of the Iceni, begins in what is now Norfolk. Rebels destroy Camulodunum (Colchester). Roman IX Legion ambushed and its infantry wiped out by the rebels. Londinium (London) sacked. Verulanium (St Albans) sacked. Somewhere in the Midlands, Roman forces commanded by Gaius Suetonius Paulinus destroy Boudicca's army.

Rather than face capture, Boudicca poisons herself and her two daughters. Romans ravage the lands of the rebel tribes and their sympathisers.

61   Gaius Suetonius Paulinus recalled from Britain.

Boudicca and history

The Roman Empire

The Italian city of Rome was founded in 753 BC.
Over the next centuries, the city grew mightier and
mightier. It began by taking over the neighbouring
lands. Powered by its mighty army and navy, it went
on to conquer other lands to the north, south, east
and west of Italy.

By the time of Emperor Augustus (27 BC – 14
AD), the Roman Empire stretched over Greece,
Spain, France, Switzerland, and much of North
Africa and the Middle East.

Wherever the Romans went, they built roads and
towns. They also brought law and order, allowing
traders to go about their business in peace.

But before we praise the Romans too highly,
we need to remember that they were ferocious,
bloodthirsty conquerors. Moreover, they kept slaves
to do their hard work. Slaves were often treated
little better than animals.

Roman Britain

Julius Caesar, a great Roman general, attacked southern Britain in 55 BC and 54 BC. He did not stay long on either occasion, and after he'd gone Britain remained outside the Roman Empire for almost 100 years.

During this time, Britons traded with the Empire, and Roman ideas became known in Britain. That is probably the way most Britons liked it – being on the edge of the Empire but not part of it. The Romans thought otherwise. Starting in 43 AD, a massive Roman army invaded Britain and soon much of the country was under its control. For the Britons, this had advantages and disadvantages. They enjoyed the law and order the Romans brought, but they had lost control of their own country. Moreover, the Romans dealt extremely harshly with anyone who did not do precisely as they said.

As far as we know, Boudicca and her husband tried to get on with their new masters. But Roman cruelty made Boudicca change her mind, with terrible consequences…

History, the search for truth

Neither of the two lawyers in this book – Tanka Bessant and Leroy Williams – tell lies. They both argue using historical facts: Roman historians wrote that Boudicca and her daughters were treated very badly, that the Queen then led an incredibly violent rebellion against the Romans, and that Gaius Suetonius Paulinus crushed this rebellion with extreme cruelty.

But history is not just knowing facts; it's about deciding how important they are and what they mean. And whether or not we can trust them. The Britons, for example, were illiterate. All the facts we have about Boudicca and her rebellion come from Roman historians. Do you think they might have played down the cruelty of Gaius Suetonius Paulinus and exaggerated the terrible deeds of Boudicca and her followers?

Life in the past was different

So, what do we make of Boudicca's behaviour? It's easy to label her a murdering butcher because of the death and destruction she was responsible for. We are horrified by the idea of destroying a town, burning all its buildings, and killing all its inhabitants.

On the other hand, we need to remember that no one invited the Romans into Britain. They conquered it by force, crushing all opposition. Few Romans thought this behaviour was wrong: they thought they were helping the Britons by giving them the benefits of Roman civilization. When Boudicca and her followers used cruelty and violence against the Romans, they didn't believe they were doing anything wrong, either. They said they were doing just what the Romans did – using force to get their way.

In short, we must guard against believing that people who lived 2,000 years ago thought as we do. Our ideas of right and wrong are not the same as theirs. Before we judge them, therefore, we must first understand how very, very different things were all that time ago.

That's what makes the study of history so fascinating.

Glossary

Archaeology:
Learning about the past by studying things that remain

Barbarian:
Rough and uncivilized; the Romans used for the word to describe someone who lived outside their empire

Conquer:
Take over a land by force

Crucify:
Execute a person by fixing them to a wooden cross and leaving them to die

Defendant:
Person in court accused of a crime

Deliberations:
Discussions

Doe:
Female deer

Dock:
Place in a courtroom where the accused person stands or sits

Empire:
Many lands under one government

Found:
To set up or establish

Horde:
Unruly mob or gang

Inferno:
Raging fire

Invade:
Attack a land with an army

Jury:
Group who decide whether an accused person is innocent or guilty

Paltry:
Tiny and feeble

Prosecutor:
Lawyer whose job is to prove to the jury that an accused person is guilty

Ravage:
Ruin or spoil with great ferocity

Sack:
Destroy a town or city and steal everything of value in it

Sacred:
Holy

Toga:
Long, loose robe worn by Roman men

Turncoat:
Traitor

Verdict:
Decision in a law court – innocent or guilty

If you enjoyed reading *Boudicca*, look out for other titles in the series.

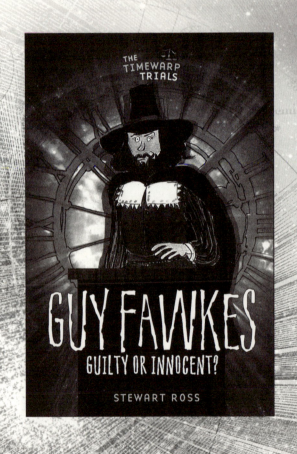

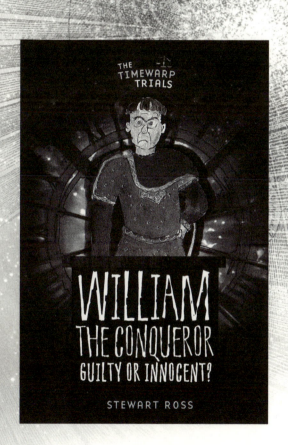

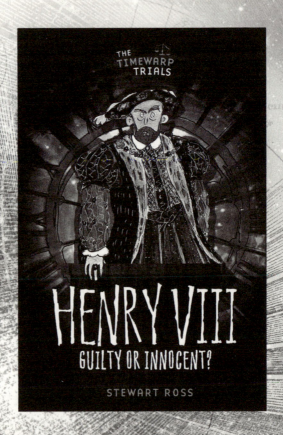